AF413521

PEOPLE IN A BOX

Everything You Need to Know about the TV

Technology for Kids
Children's Reference & Nonfiction

Speedy Publishing LLC

40 E. Main St. #1156

Newark, DE 19711

www.speedypublishing.com

Copyright 2017

In this book, we're going to talk about the technology behind the invention of television. So, let's get right to it!

With television, you have the world at your fingertips. Just a click on your remote makes it possible for you to watch a sports event thousands of miles away, to listen to the President give a speech, or to see a caravan traveling across the Sahara desert. The advent of television completely changed the way people were being educated and entertained.

Multimedia video wall television

Today, most kids watch about 1,000 hours of television every year. That's more time than they spend in school, which is about 900 hours yearly. Many parents don't think it's good for kids to watch so much television. In fact, one of the inventors of the television, Philo T. Farnsworth, wouldn't let his kids watch the "talking box" that he had helped invent, because he thought the programming was too mindless. No matter whether you think television is helpful or harmful to society, you have to admit it's an amazing invention!

THE VERY FIRST TELEVISION

In 1926, John Logie Baird, a Scottish inventor demonstrated a new machine to a group of people in London, England. He had taken everyday objects like a tin for cookies and lights from a bicycle to construct a mechanical television set. At the core of his mechanical television was a quickly spinning disk. It was made from the top of a hat box!

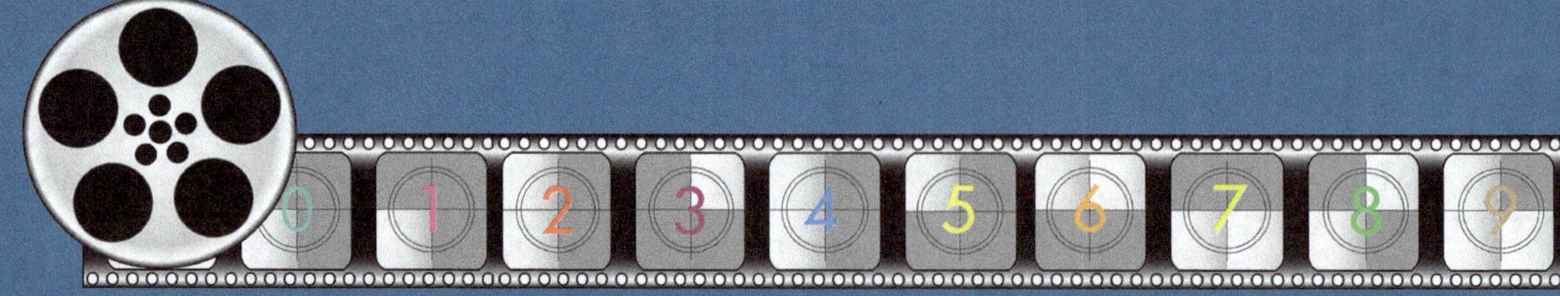

John Logie Baird

LONDON COUNTY COUNCIL
IN 1926
IN THIS HOUSE
JOHN LOGIE
BAIRD
1888 - 1946
FIRST DEMONSTRATED
TELEVISION

John Logie Baird Blue Plaque

Although the first moment a face was seen on television was historic, Baird's pictures were so unclear that his invention wasn't practical.

Several years later, Vladimir Zworykin, a Russian-American inventor made improvements on the cathode-ray tube. The tube was used to show pictures on a screen. By using the cathode-ray tube, he created a television that worked electronically, not mechanically.

cathode ray tube

retro old television from 70's

The earliest televisions had enormous boxes with tiny screens and only showed black and white displays. The television you have at home more than likely uses digital technology instead of the old-fashioned cathode-ray tube.

HOW DOES A TELEVISION WORK?

Prior to the beginning of television, people used to sit in front of their radios at home to listen to a news broadcast or program. Television expanded this experience by adding pictures to the sounds of radio. Radios send sounds through the air by using radio waves. Radio waves are invisible electromagnetic waves.

They travel in the air at the same speed as light, which is 186,282 miles per second. Imagine a surfer riding on waves in the ocean. Information, in this case, both pictures and sound, travel on top of these radio waves to show up on your television screen.

Television is a complicated invention and many different inventors contributed to its creation. There are three different components that make a television work:

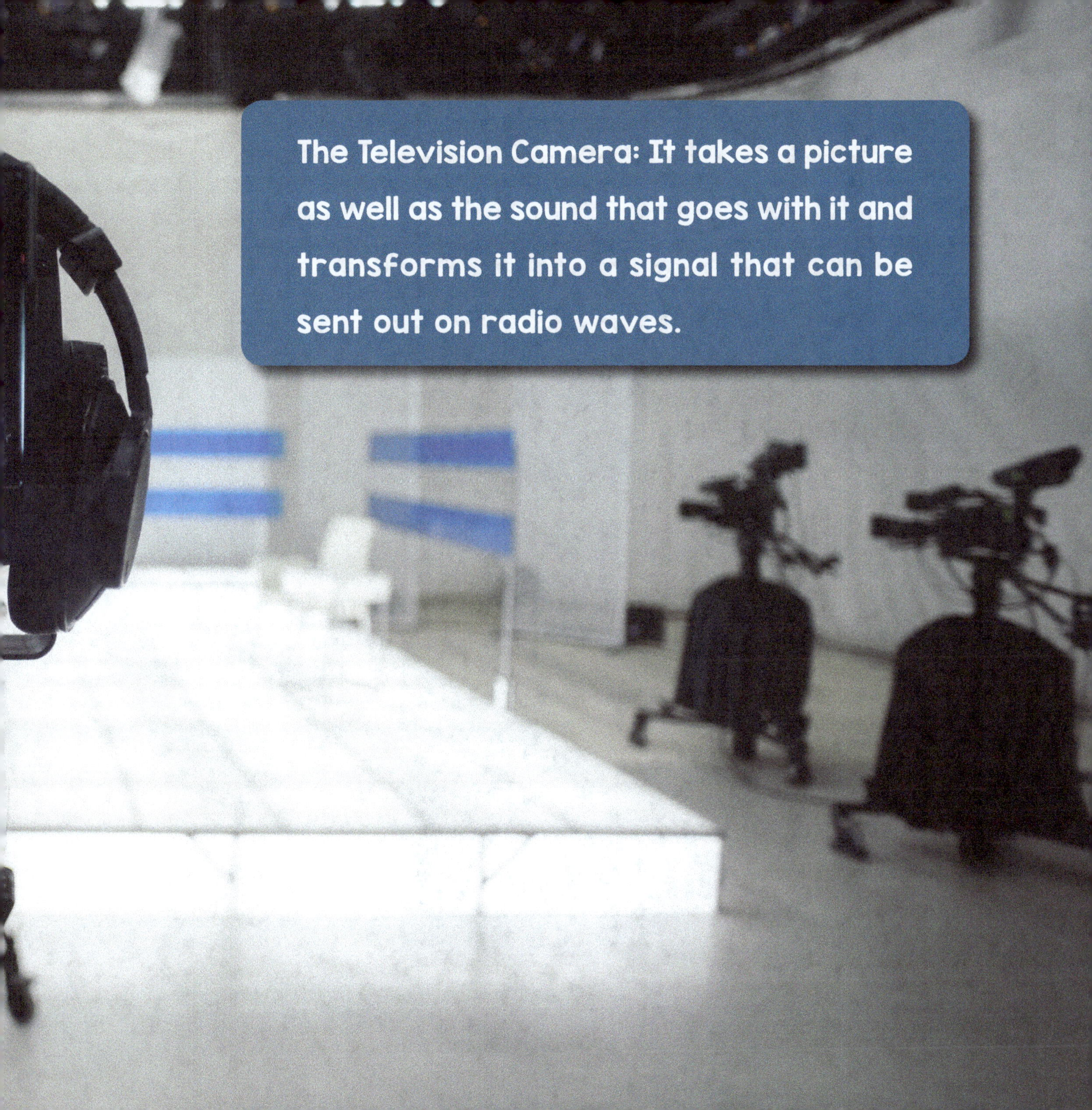
The Television Camera: It takes a picture as well as the sound that goes with it and transforms it into a signal that can be sent out on radio waves.

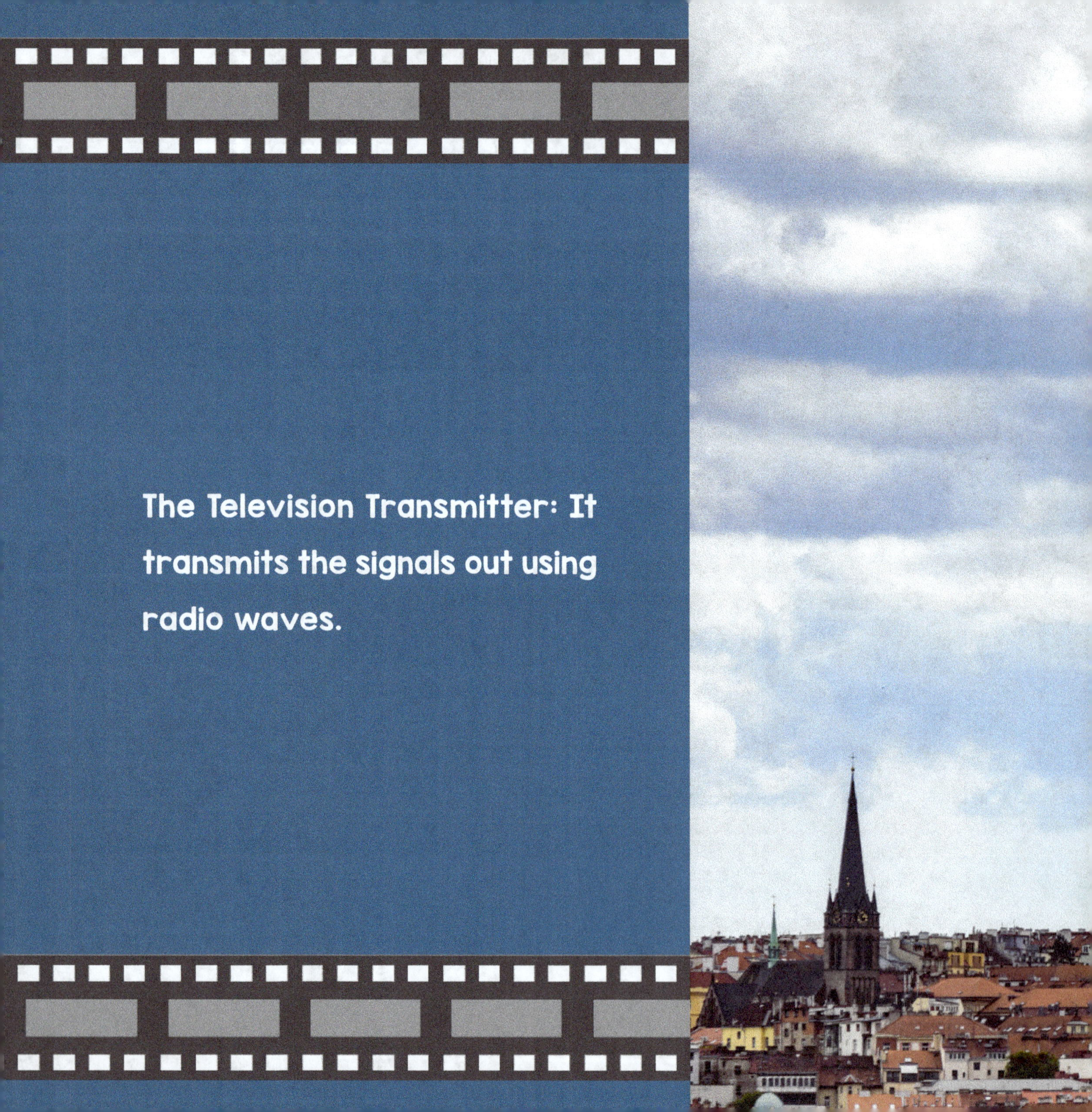

The Television Transmitter: It transmits the signals out using radio waves.

Zizkov Television Tower Prague

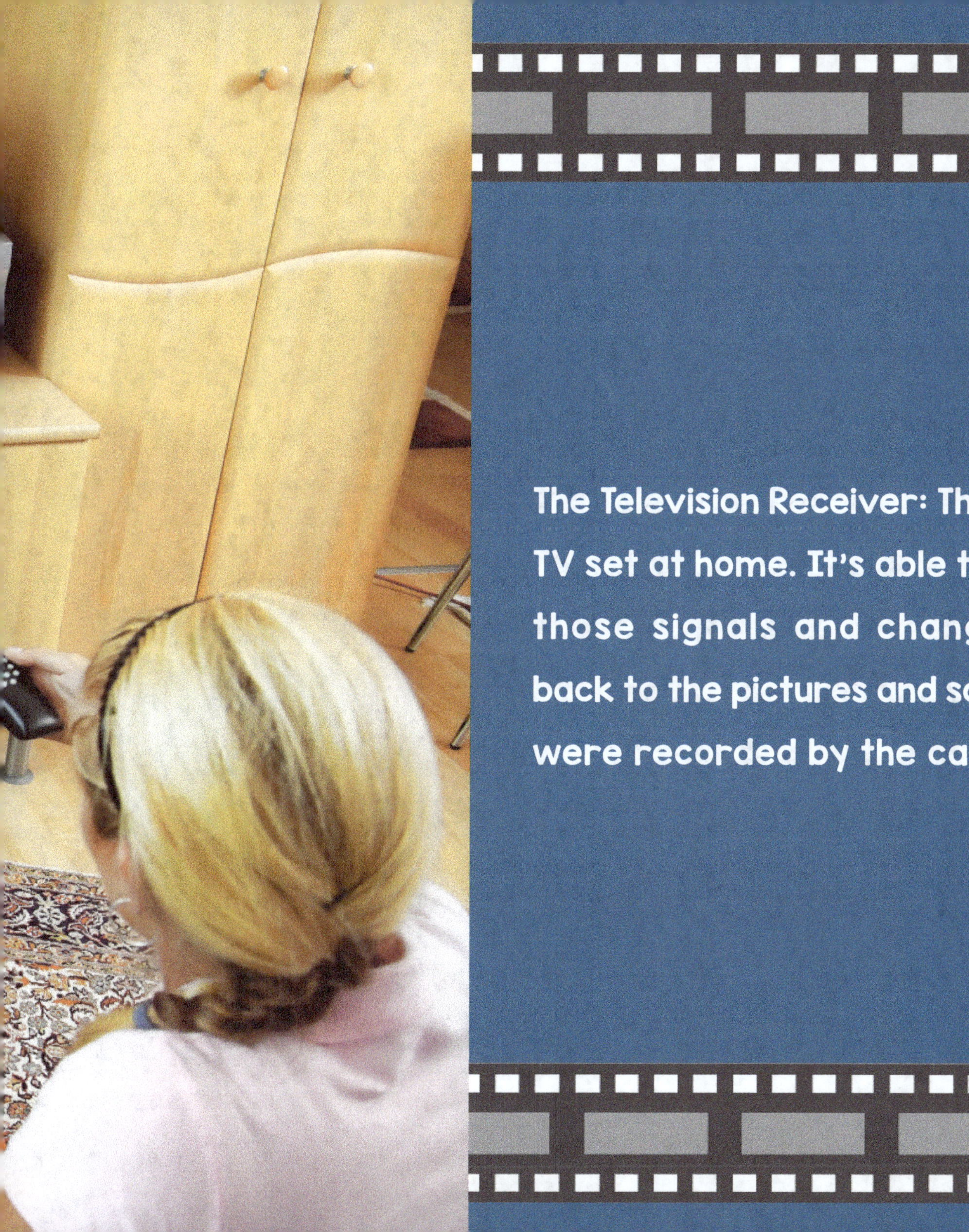

The Television Receiver: This is your TV set at home. It's able to accept those signals and change them back to the pictures and sound that were recorded by the camera.

Have you ever flipped the pages of a flipbook? Each page has an individual image, but when you flip the pages rapidly, it looks like a moving image. Television does something similar. It transmits still pictures to your eyes so quickly one after the other that they appear to be in motion. There are different rates that are used, but the least amount of pictures it transmits in just one second is 24.

That means there are 24 different still pictures being sent to your eyes in just one second when you are watching a television screen! The images are being sent so fast that your brain just blends them into a picture that's moving. Television is similar to a giant flipbook that works electronically.

HOW DOES A TELEVISION CAMERA WORK?

Light is reflected into our eyes so we can see things. If you were taking a photo with an old-fashioned camera, you could snap a picture by using film that is sensitive to light. It would capture the light on film that would show how an object or person or scene looked exactly at the moment you took the shot.

Television Camera

Digital Camera

A digital camera does this too, except it doesn't use film. It just captures and saves that moment electronically. A television camera captures new pictures at a rate of at least 24 pictures every second to give the illusion of a picture that's moving.

On a digital camera, you look at a display to see how your finished shot will look. A television cameraman doesn't look through the lens of the TV camera. Instead, he looks at a screen that shows an image of what the lens is "seeing."

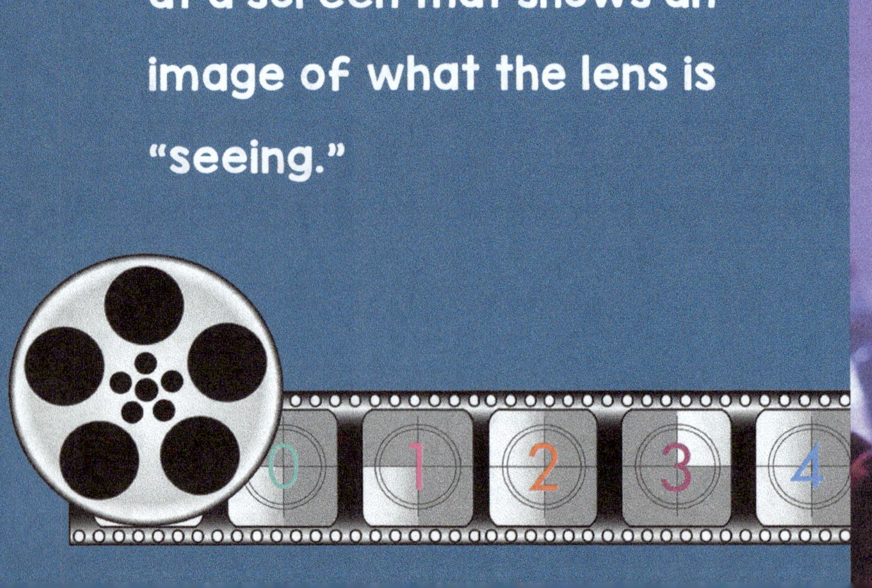

HOW DOES A TELEVISION CAMERA TAKE A PICTURE?

Suppose that you wanted to copy a masterpiece that you saw on an art gallery wall. You could take a sheet of paper and divide it up using squares. This grid would help you to concentrate on each section of the piece of art that you wanted to copy. You could work from the top to the bottom or from the left side to the right side.

In order to transform a picture into a radio signal that can be broadcast, a television camera copies the scene a line at a time. There are detectors inside the camera that sense the light across the picture and scan it line by line just like your eyes scan the text in a book.

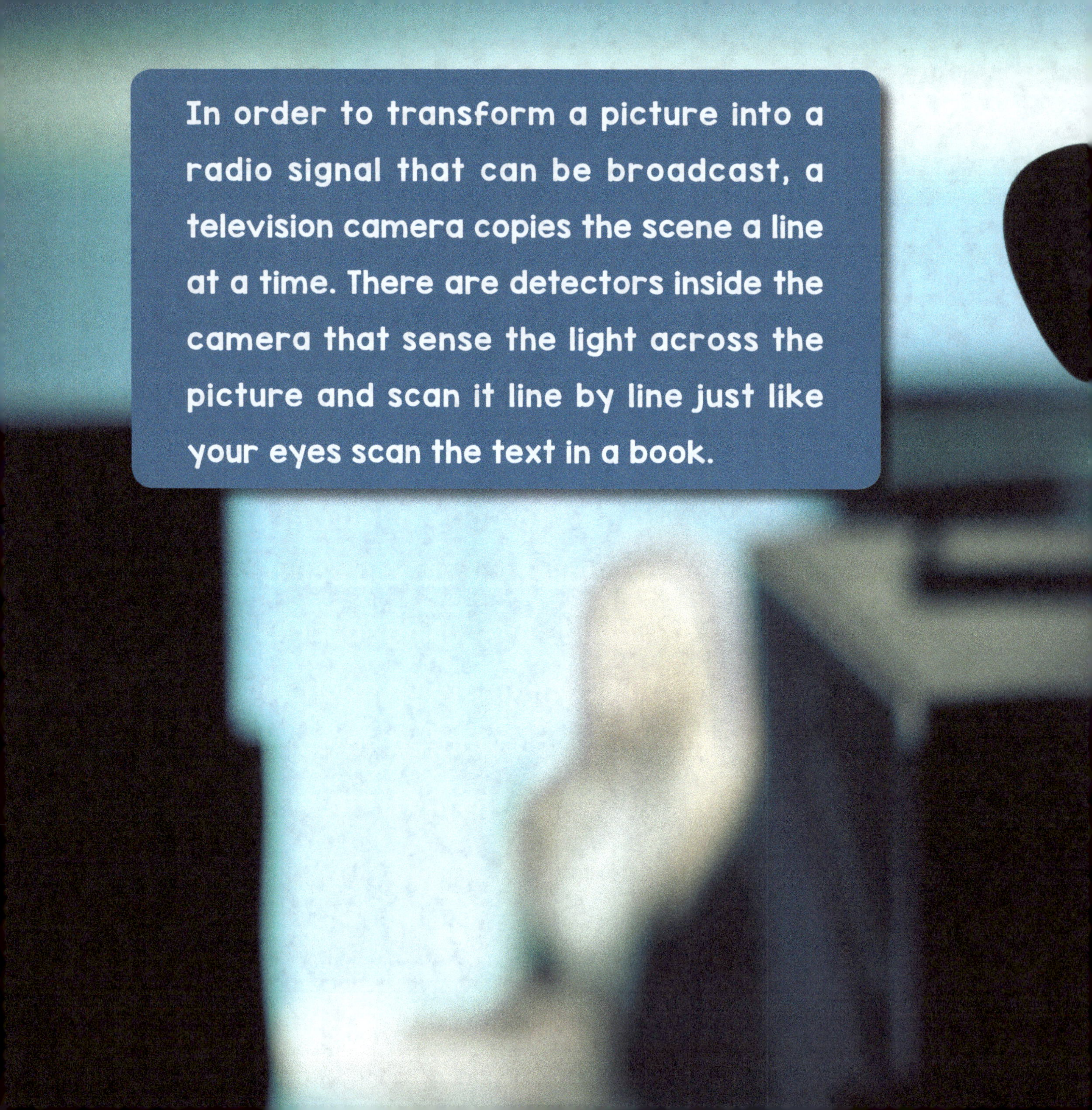

The process transforms each image into 525 lines of light that have varying colors. The images are beamed using radio waves that travel through the air and arrive at your home television as a video signal. Along with these images, microphones record the sounds that go with the images. The audio signal is sent separately with the picture information.

HOW DOES A TELEVISION TRANSMITTER WORK?

Suppose you were playing in the backyard and you wanted your friend in the yard next door to hear you. You would shout at him as loudly as possible so he could hear your voice. Louder sounds make larger waves. Those larger waves can travel a greater distance before they get absorbed by houses, trees, or whatever other objects are in the environment.

transmitter tower parabolas

Television Tower

Radio waves behave in a similar way. To make strong radio waves that have the ability to carry pictures as well as sounds, you need a very strong transmitter. This transmitter would have to send the signal from the TV station to someone's home television set. The transmitter is like an enormous antenna that is located on the peak of a hill so it can send the signals out over long distances.

However, your home might not receive television signals in this way. There are two other ways you could be receiving your signals. If you have cable in your home, your television pictures are transmitted via a special cable called a fiber-optic cable.

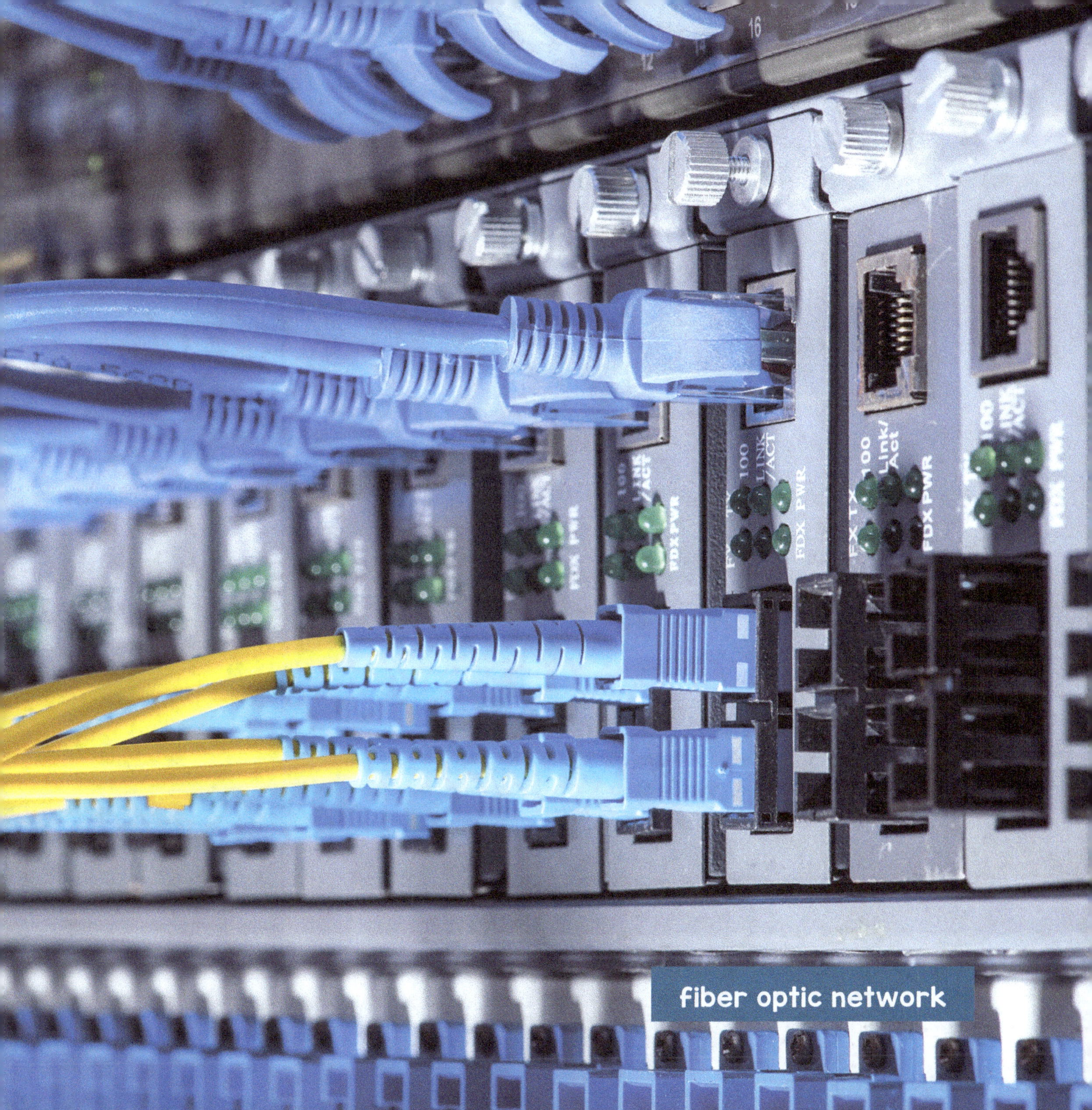
fiber optic network

satellite dish

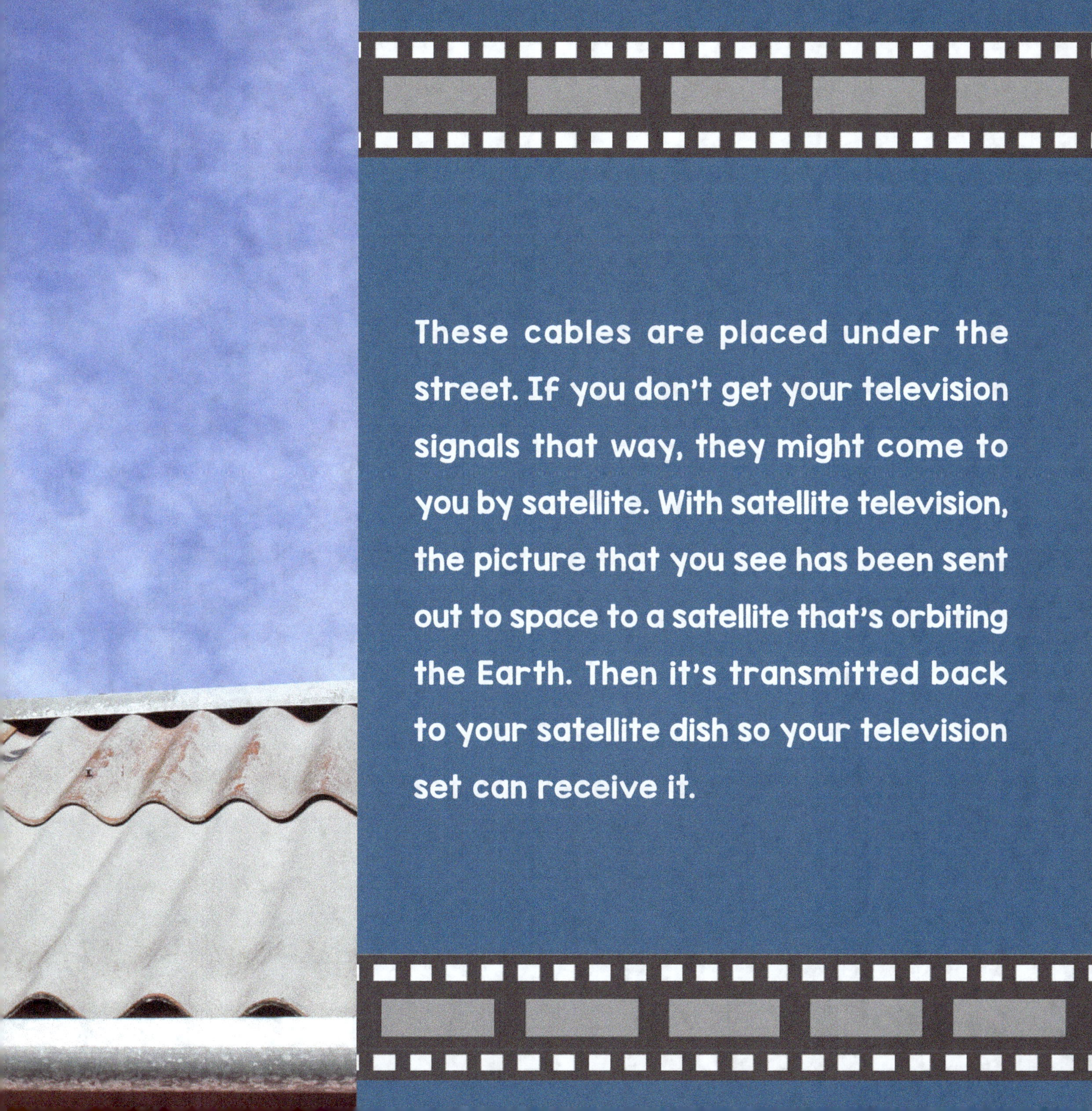

These cables are placed under the street. If you don't get your television signals that way, they might come to you by satellite. With satellite television, the picture that you see has been sent out to space to a satellite that's orbiting the Earth. Then it's transmitted back to your satellite dish so your television set can receive it.

Originally, most television broadcasts were sent with analog signals. The signals were sent in a wave that was moving up and down. However, lots of countries are in the process of switching to television that's broadcast digitally, similar to the way that digital radio is broadcast. The signals are sent in a numerical code. More programs can be transmitted this way and the quality of the picture is actually better because the signals aren't at risk from interference.

satellite dish and TV antenna

HOW DOES A TELEVISION RECEIVER WORK?

It really doesn't make any difference which way your television set receives the television signal. It can come from an underground cable, an antenna or aerial on the roof, or a satellite dish in your yard. No matter what way it comes in, your television will still use the same process to show the picture to you. It basically does the exact opposite that the television camera does.

SUMMARY

Many different inventors contributed to the invention of television as we know it today. Television needs three separate components to work: the television camera, the television transmitter, and the television receiver. The television camera captures a scene in 24 or more pictures per second. That scene is transformed into a signal using 525 lines of light in varying colors. The television cameraman doesn't look into a lens when he films. Instead, he sees a screen that displays what the camera is "seeing."

television cameraman

CAM 2
CAM 3
CAM 4
CAM 5
CAM RED 1
CAM RED 2
LIN 2
LIN 3
LIN 4
television station

Next, the signal travels from the television station or from wherever the cameras are capturing the image to your home television set. Those signals can be sent to your home through a powerful antenna transmitter, or by fiber-optic cables that are buried underground, or by beaming them out in space to a satellite that beams them back. No matter how your television receives the signal, it then converts it back into an image you can see on your screen so that you can watch your favorite television program! It also sends the audio signal at the same time so you can hear the program too.

Now that you know more about the technology behind television you may want to find out more about the development of video games in the Baby Professor book The Multi-Billion Dollar Industry of Computers and Video Games.

SOURCE
1
2
3
4
5
6
7
8
9
TTX/MIX
0
PRE-CH
MUTE
CH LIST
P
MENU
SMART
HUB
GUIDE
TOOLS
INFO

Visit

BABY PROFESSOR
EDUCATION KIDS

www.BabyProfessorBooks.com

to download Free Baby Professor eBooks
and view our catalog of new and exciting
Children's Books